BABELDOM

Talal Alyan

Astrophil Press
at University of South Dakota
2019

Copyright © 2018 by Talal Alyan
Cover art by Grant Riedel
Layout and design by duncan b. barlow
Additional Proofreading by Sabrina Kelly

Astrophil Press at University of South Dakota
1st pressing 2019

Library of Congress Cataloging-in-Publication Data
Talal Alyan 1991–
Babeldom/Talal Alyan
          p. cm.
    ISBN 978-0-9980199-1-8 (pbk. : paper)
     1.Poetry, American
Library of Congress Control Number: 2018951632

http://www.astrophilpress.com

babeldom: a state of noisy confusion resembling that at Babel

I

II

Acknowledgements:

The Wax Paper: 'Apocalypse,' 'Late Hour,' and 'Off Script'
Mud Season Review: 'Manifest Destiny' 'Locust' and 'Fallout'
Origins Journal: 'Men and Their Masters'
Literary Juice: 'Separate Bedrooms'
After Happy Hour Review: 'Prayer' and 'Red'
Black Fox Literary Magazine: 'How I Got Sober,' and 'Tourist'
Tipton Poetry Journal: 'Zodiac'
Birch Gang Review: 'Tournament'

for my family

I

Glasswork

maybe it's 1982. a woman
has just set down the phone
receiver. she looks out at
Portland, the patch light and
cold apartments. through her
window she peers into the
frame of a living room. a man
on a plastic chair, the only
furniture in the room.

what is it you would say, she mutters to
herself.

the man hears only the static
of the space heater. dimly looks
at his suitcase and back at the
plaster wall. he thinks of his
mother, her quiet dorm in a
nursing home. he debates
whether he should call.

by now, he decides, *she will
have fallen asleep*.

the mother has meanwhile
sat quietly in her bed for
an hour. the lights are no
longer on. it is regulation.
she thinks of a house near a
cul-de-sac, its rooms warm with
sleeping bodies. the kitchen light
still glowing. rubbing spices into a
chicken breast, a middle-aged
version of herself stands over
the counter.

she laughs to herself, puncturing the
daydream,

you kept saying you wanted to
rest.

the nurses start to enter the room to
calm the woman. other residents
begin to wake.

how could you have known, she keeps laughing,
how could you have ever known?

Prayer

this winter premiers with pickaxe and pneumonia. he climbs out of sleep like a window, curls his arms across a naked mattress, keeps his eyes shut and pleads: *return what is mine*. this is how he barters. this is how each day greets him: with theft.

the weather recast in front of him. It is December and he had no idea. although beneath the overpass he can explain what came before this: roar, arc light, tremor. all the milestones lining the curbside, spoiled and sheer. *be delicate*, he whispers, *they are clues*.

it is two decades prior. there was a surgery removing his tonsils. the boy lie recovering on a sofa watching Aladdin. in his periphery he sees his sister outside, playing flash tag in the dark with the neighborhood children. he turns his head, watches their figures rushing across the backyard.

the man, now seated on a bench, closes his eyes—*return to me, return to me*—the whiteness of his sister's sneakers, even a faded purple shirt she once owned, reappears with such clarity. he hears their thrilled voices, the sharp ring of her prepubescent laughter against the warmth of the television color.

show me a man who knows better than to search for what is lost, to forgo the toil of this prayer: the arch of his back, a galaxy of scrambling fingers.

Men and Their Masters

this our harvest of African rice. ingrown sprout
with wild dirt.

this   the jaundice-eyed labor of men in
castoff rags.

this the monsoon that
will arrive in half a week.

the men daring not stare
into that fog   walk vigilant in the field row carved for them.

this the wail
of kettle pot   its belly blended with fine molasses.

the landlord looking with
boredom at the sky,
remarking to himself

that the storm
will help his crop.

some men insist
that they are chosen
some men swear
they are just   being tested.

each goes to bed every night
with this contract

each with pity
for the other.

The Men That Left Town

an airliner descends on a tarmac in Kansas City. the asphalt still gleaming from a rainstorm that ended an hour before it landed. a man in his late thirties looks out from the middle seat towards the window. he thinks of the four men that are waiting inside the arrival terminal. it has been a decade since he left to a bigger city to find there was nothing to find. the plane continues to taxi. he pictures the walk towards the baggage claim, that black carrousel dropping his luggage from a vent, the red string he tied to its handle. or the handle between his fingers as he pulls its weight behind him, the arrival sign glowing over the arch of the exit. maybe he will say—quietly—when the faces of his friends appear, that home is where the heart is. and in his heart, he will mean: the surest way to corrupt a dream is to stalk it

Libretto

the sunlight emerges abruptly from the Manhattan skyline.
it slips into the room, illuminates
the desk that you sit on.

you get up mechanically, leave the apartment then
the building. begin to walk towards the water.

the railing is discolored,
covered in rust and grime. you climb over it. your palms
hold the metal. you look out at the East River.

a crowd gathers around you. some take out their phones and
record the scene, others approach and ask what you are
doing. more people arrive, and by now they are pleading with
you, begging you not to jump.

a man with a thick Brooklyn accent shouts out
that you should want to live.

the water tosses itself.

it looks like the first body you've ever seen.

Spoils

all that was untaken at the Spanish port: drums of vinegar and baitfish. the last fisherman returns to harbor with no catch. it has been two weeks like this. he moors his small boat and gathers the equipment into a gray haversack, rehearses in his mind what he will say to his wife.

the two barrels sit on the boardwalk. the fisherman notices and quietly looks around, kicks gently at the casks. the man is not a thief, has only stolen once before, a few coins from his mother's purse when he was a child; he sobbed his confession four days later. he tells himself these are gifts. or orphans; that they will go to waste. he repeats this chorus to himself as he loads them into his truck, begins the drive home.

his wife asks no questions. she peers into the casks with excitement as he opens them with a crowbar. the odor—sharp and sour—fills the room, the man staring at the spoils of his theft, too ashamed to look at his wife. but she dances around the room, declares the fish can be pickled in vinegar and eaten as a delicacy, muses aloud about recipes, begins boiling water in the kitchen. the man is grateful for his wife's mercy, the display of excitement.

they eat the same meal for dinner and breakfast: pickled fish in its own broth and stale bread. each time, the wife moans in pleasure with every bite, repeating to her husband that this is a delicacy in many villages. he plays along, licks his fingers clean every time. the recital continues until, one day, the man goes out to sea and does not return.

for a month, family and friends and strangers arrive at her door, offering condolences, bringing with them plates of food. the whole house is crammed with their offerings; the woman is forced to stack plates in her bedroom.

in the mornings, she washes her face. before anyone has the chance to knock on her door, she sneaks into the refrigerator, pulls out from behind that ocean of food a single bowl, dips old bread into that sour, rotting broth, moans through her closed mouth.

Terminal

the punch line is that everyone
got in.

there was no waiting room or
court. no bearded judge to review
the cinema of your life. the only
gates were the ones that surrounded
the housing complexes.

it was simply
like waking up
again.

families reunited. old lovers
found. friends catching up with
the ones that departed too early.

the new arrivals sat waiting at the
terminal. they studied the arrival
boards for the name of a son or a
wife or a mother until that person
finally appeared. then together
waited for another.

the houses only
grew fuller.

Locust

interpret the tusks of
this journey:

a locust jolts itself
from the sink, hovers
erratically between the
tile walls of the
bathroom

a forewing mangled in
the ambush. the insect
bucks in a jar-pen,
thudding against the
glass.

off in search of
swarm—she tells herself when

finally she releases
her palm, shakes
the jar out the
window;

she does not see the
plummet, its wing
contorted batting
in vain or the body
spasms once it
lands on the
ground.

oh glory of
our lord,
the mercy of giants.

Miracles

this is the last miracle.

holiday lights along the windows of a
convenience store off I-78. you pick out a
frozen meatloaf from the fridge. the clerk
places it in a dirty microwave behind the
counter. it spins for two minutes before he
removes it, his fingers protected with a
brown napkin. you thank him as he scatters
dimes into your palm.

in the parking lot, you sit with the moan of the
car heater. the oil from the meat seeps through
the plastic bag and onto the pants you have been
wearing since last Tuesday.

the food waits in your lap. something is
missing. the plastic silverware, and something
else—maybe you aren't hungry or unsure
where it is you want to arrive. you try to focus
on the hunger: it brought you here, off the
highway.

what would it be you would long for if
you could stand to long for anything
anymore?

you chew the unsalted meat. it tastes like foil.
periodically, you reach for a bottle of water, flush the
work of your teeth into your stomach.

each time it happens, you are grateful.
answers to a prayer you haven't yet made.

Afterhours

rumor has it
the boys lined belladonna
in a hurricane glass,

sipped the mocktail,
taking turns in an apartment
that had been
foreclosed.

three of them were sent to the emergency room.
only one
died.

he had skipped breakfast.

the poison went
through him like white milk.
turned his bowels
into asp.

all they found beneath the sheet was hoarfrost
and trapped air.

child's play.

Zodiac

I.

rubs
vapor rub into the skin above
her neckline. the odor of
peppermint rises into her
nostrils like a plume. it opens
her sinuses for the first time in
four days.

outside
this city has the magic of a
summer. she picks up her
laundry hamper and dumps
it onto the floor, scavenges
for a garment clean enough
to wear, discovers a cocktail
dress with a blemish on the
collar, stands over the sink
and scours it with steel wool.

squeezes
her feet into a pair of black
stilettos. the mirror offers a
yellowed version of herself. she
tosses her hair. displeased by
how little her appearance
changes, decides to just leave
the house

II.

swallows
a caplet of klonopin to calm his

nerves. the tap water that he uses
to wash it down is warm. he sits on
the sofa, lists the state capitals in
his mind as he waits for the
medicine to work. it hits him like
faith.

inside
the rear seats of a
taxi, the cab television
projects the monologue of
a late-night host into his face.
he fumbles with the screen,
trying to mute its noise.

dries
his eyes against the back of his
sleeve. he squints to shelter them
from the wind. it doesn't help.
they continue to well.

III.

downtown
lights in a city big enough
to be a universe. the restaurant
in which they meet was chosen
by a mutual friend. the glassware is
smeared with the fingerprints of the
busboy. they sit at the table, recite
their names and professions.

he
tells her he doesn't really do this
sort of thing. she nervously laughs,
tries to conceal that she has taken offense.

the waiter brings garlic bread sticks and
soda water. he gropes in his pocket, his
fingers looking for mints, afraid the garlic
will stick to his breath.

they
both order the same dish. it is linguini
in a bed of white clam sauce. it drips
from her fork as she nods along to his
stories from college. towards her last
few bites, she begins to panic, worries
that she has been too shy. she decides
to try something new.

she tells a story from childhood,
how she used to be scared that the
house her family moved into when she
was in middle school was haunted, tells
him that for those first two weeks in that
new house, the only way she was able to
fall asleep was to picture the world as an
aquatic kingdom: a fiction of glow fish
and tentacles and coral reef.

after she finishes talking, she notices no reaction
in his expression and quietly changes the
subject.

they say goodnight. both return to their buildings,
then their apartments then their rooms and drift
into sleep.

she dreams of neon jellyfish;
he does
as well.

Off Script

forsake the narrator – rambling and dull –
      let us try something new: you walk
      to the other side of the city with
      a static in your head. it takes
      everything you have to not tell
      yourself that this is the beginning
      of a story. wait—you've done it
      again. you're doing it now.

just the rush of images. this world is not
      your novel. just the petroleum
      jelly on your lip, the bloated
      abdomen tucked in jeans. the
      copper keychain from your
      sister that impales your thigh,
      only that throbbing and nothing
      else. just the south-east Asian
      store clerk that hands you back
      your debit card over a pack of
      cigarettes that you've bought—
      not his family, or that look in his
      face that tells you nothing but
      the beginning of some plot that
      you construct in your mind. not
      his mother shouting for him over
      a long-distance phone call in a
      language you can't conjure, not
      that first silence when the credit
      runs out and the line cuts. not
      that clench in his gut when he
      wonders if she'll die before he gets
      a chance to call her back.

just the soft air of this Tuesday,
      on your neck
      and wrist. only that.

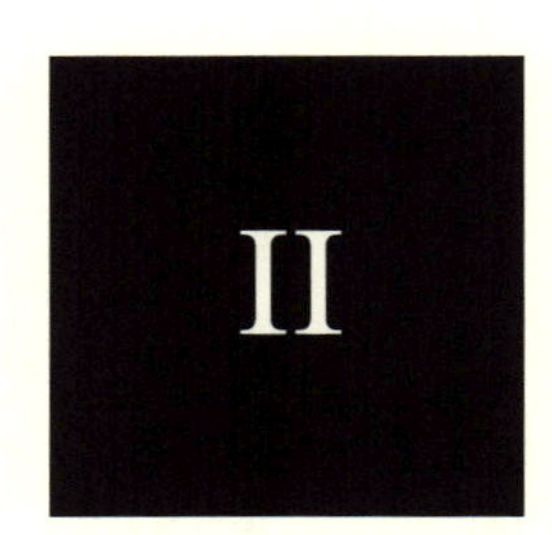
II

Stand-up Philosophy

a circle of light
cast against the
figure of a body
that holds in one
hand a microphone
trailing into a
snake of wires
that ends at a
speaker

       and speaks:
       here is what
       I came to say

       here is what
       you'll hear:

Native

      our inheritance:

chemical silos and strip malls,
     the ugly pink   omens
of a Midwestern fatherland.

this now ritual:

     coil our forearm in
the practice of worship
or surrender,

whichever will calm the spite of our
maker.

see, this
     corn crib in a
dull season   barren as dust bowl.

we are in a way pilgrims, too.

     collecting
bare husks in our paunch,
dry idols   gifts.

understand:

our contempt is
native
     to this land.

Red

I.

if you want to be heard, push
against the black
curtains that whip
across the windowpane

swing until you fall
fall until you land
and when you land:

red plains inside a world
of no beasts,
no rhythm but your
own

throbbing across the high grass.

II.

if you want to be seen, do
it in dark light.
sharp teeth exposed
to an audience or
the camera of a lover

that will keep
it in a tin box for a dozen
years.

it will sit in a landfill:

brittle red
metal

powdered into hail.

Sutras

aphid   lift the baby blue caplet
from the window sill

let it dissolve
          in soda water with
lime extract. if this is too tart,
use cherry.

instruct your
stomach   bloated and sore to
welcome this.

lay on your side with radio-purr
and tinsel. wear a sleep mask
          like a shackle.

when the radiator spits out
steam

pretend to be
in the subtropics.

Manifest Destiny

"…..grow to love that strange language" — Sujata Bhatt

this century
bores.   it growls
          a feral beast.

I want to devour it
with silver-spoon
teeth. put sea salt
along the spinal
cord of its borders
with bullets and
ammonia.   war of men
                                war of metal
                                more of

the cult king that struts in rags. under his belt
a creole tongue and the spices of another continent—

on this
side of the axis,   the victors all dead.

give me
a different history

a new inheritance.

the canvas of an America
that hasn't been touched.

Screening

reel of thin film – the footage is
all cigar holed and hush. belong to

the red seat,   American retro –
kernel molar   we in audience
                     swindlers.

this is
our cinema

this is how the clippings end:

a dateline.   a soda gulp.
a paper moth
damp in the
center.

a chemistry of lights.

Tournament

display in the forecourt
of a Roman naked only
from the waist below

and it is only known
that he is from Rome
by the plaque
under the sculpture

and there must be
in a shallow grave
somewhere east
soil of the hand
that carved this

and it must look
no different than
the dirt kicked
by a boy on
vacation with his
family in
the Lazio
countryside

who speculates
this boredom is
what it must
feel like
to live forever

Sonata

I.

little black bones, tell me secrets of the heart

rot in the center
of a fruit sold on
a stand in a city.

a redbird under
the railing of
a road that circles
a mountain.

this is the fortune of the
dead.

a lifetime of gazing at stars. we watch from here

they watch from below
or above.
or neither.

amen.

II.

dark echo, river of mud.
a four-gun salute.

anywhere else
this is treason.

it is simple:

if the men talk to
captors,
the daughters all wear green.

III.

pinwheels against
a pink sky,

a wedding.   a shotgun apartment
ten months of spectacle:

what we wish for under a
new year, what we whimper
during last call.

we all do the same.
it's easy,

place your cheekbone on the floor,
let that sharp cold
fill you.

Separate Bedrooms

on my collar   the lipstick
slur of a
diabetic woman

in her handbag
sugar substitute and   foundation

this is our final lore:

pine cube. dead tooth.
entrée of snout.

I, groom   you in wig

knowing no war
will come

as   savage
as the one that
already

expects
us.

Appetite

for lunch
palatines   left-over
fingerlings, pared in April
by the housemaid.

you ask for something more,
for naked grapes to press
between the fork and
plate.

the nectar bulging
from the tines
will be garnish. it isn't enough.

never mind the fruit. try this:

pull mucus from
oysters, let its odor confuse the room.
it will travel your throat
like an oil slick. you remain
hungry.

now, bulk.

raw cauliflower in a sea of white
cream. meat lumps uncooked—
still frozen at core.

tear open that
cellophane wrap, unthawed
pink flesh that you welcome
whole.

and if you choke
don't startle. instead
whistle through
whichever cavity has
yet to betray you.

it will feel like
the world
is suddenly not
so big.

it will feel like
you have finally done
something

Elevator

no ceremony,
no altar boys,

champagne flute
orchestra.

only this: muzak, rail jaw,
tourism of the
ratite.

what I want is for my life
to conclude like a sitcom:

bare. laugh-tracked.

no cable drum. the clatter of
metal unto metal. hauled
into nightfall without
notice.

rather, this:

a man enfolded with water
a water dancing into drain
a drain—
gentle, playful,

laughing
with you.

Fallout

that first spring without us.

the footprint will remain   for a
while: hollow architecture, network
of telephone poles, asphalt still glued
to the soil.

the countryside goes first. those
fragile homes might
only take a decade
to wilt. the croplands
even less.

livestock will wait tethered.
those that survive summer will
not make it past
winter.

the cities will follow.

the grandest of them
may sit a century.

what takes our
place finds in a ghost email
an album of photographs

it studies the faces
and feels
next to nothing.

Tourist

try it this way
from outside an
interstate in a
used car that
you drove in
from Dallas

exit the rental
on the side
of a highway
then walk until
your legs give
way to the
weight of
your body.

the skin
over both
kneecaps
caked in
mud.

pray to all the gods.
the ones before you
and the ones
after.

Apocalypse

this is
how I want the curtain to close:

a hailstorm of dark meteor, the
heart of old universe

exploding into ours.

a pink month

of
sunless
glow.

red moss across
the blackwood nation.

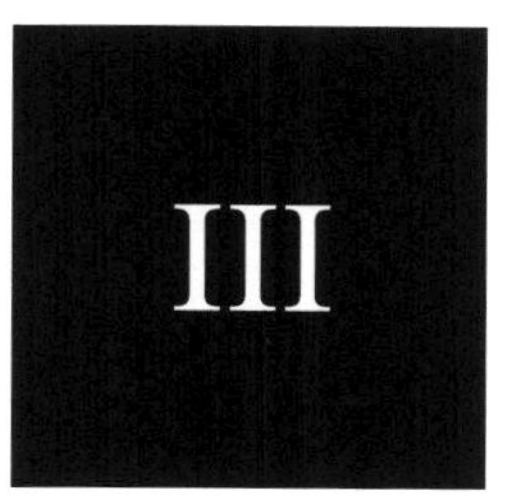
III

Year of Whiskey

I won't tell you about the raspy talk of afterlife and
mornings after, the lounge singer glancing into the
spotlight, nervously or how I felt, well, decidedly
hysteric with a shotgun laugh and wisterias in my breast
pocket, or the girl I left in Houston. *be careful, alright?*

I can still trace the progression: scarlet to smoke
to the late-shift waitress who offers remnants of
graceland to her patrons for last call;
better men than I forfeit dreams for blowjobs in
the same world that misplaced Alex Sellen.

and who is still convinced of the prospect of Los
Angeles? like love on two-bit factory wine, the
reluctant heart that sneers at 4:30 in the morning, a
stenograph of conversations you'd only ever hear in
Reno. beyond me or you or anyone we might have
met in that hotel lobby, gambling on Mama's dollar,
lurching beneath the dull constellations of San Francisco

or perhaps I am mistaken about the pale laughter
that rises from the south, how magnolias grow towards
their makers, the stereo circa 1926 that told us of the flood.
I always find my heart breaking for June and the lonely men
at diners with nowhere to go except home.

Late Hour

"…until at last I lift you up and wrap you within me" —Stephen Dobyns

think of the moon   —not as some ornament
                        in the sky. or a gloom
                        that hangs over your
                        bedroom in the late
                          hours—

           think of its
           pale skin the
           way you would
           a woman in a
           green dress.

           her shoulders
           perked on a
           backless stool
           stirring a
           glass of gin.

           that same distance
           that same thirst

like a woman in a green dress
leaving the bar.

Weekends

all of this metropolis folded into the
window of a car on the FDR.

I thought I knew well this return alone. the
flood lights. the carpet slant. a quiet that
won't move.

the following day—I begin to
assemble myself from scratch.
cast salt until I lie and lie
better.

Questions to Ask on a First Date

what do you do
what do you tell yourself
in the poor lighting before
dusk when you cannot
sleep but cannot
tolerate either the
matchstick strike
of waiting for night
who do you hope
will hear when you
murmur that this season
has betrayed you, so
sure were you of
a fresh break that
you shelved the
eulogy, why do you still
resurface just to
pick up the mass
of your body, patiently
slide both legs
into underwear
then pants then
shoes

how will you manage
on the loud subway
ride back to Queens
to the story
you have written and read
every day
for thirty years.

Poem for Alex

you knew I wrote poems although back then I wasn't really writing much of anything or doing much of anything except drinking away months and talking so much shit that it's a wonder I made it out of that city with my neck intact and I would call you Wednesdays and ask if you were coming out and you'd say something about having work the next morning though inevitably you'd come and we'd order vodka martinis and shots of whiskey, pay full price and smoke cigarettes with every stranger drunk enough to listen and I swear the truth, the solemn truth, was before Lauren finally confessed over the phone that you had died I couldn't tell if she was laughing or sobbing.

Lullaby

a cherry tree above an ancient city or
a city inside the hollow of a seed or

another night where I sleep-run past the
borders of a country like it was the yellow
tape at the end of a race or

I would settle for the milk of
a new crop. the African violet of
a nightmare sky

or even a wind that lurches
like a god. a roar that
flushes the red from
my face.

or
a nocturne that puts me so
deeply to sleep that I sleep
and I sleep and I
see the colors
of that world
with the eyes
of this one.

Intermission

every morning for a week
I have woken with the same terror.

between the living room and my bedroom,
I travel in a grey bathrobe across the expanse
of a few feet, telling myself that morning
is not an enemy.

and I have given up whiskey.
and I have given up red meat.
kneeled for our Lord before a
bedspring pulpit

to no avail.

on a red-eye Tuesday
sputtering into sleep like a coward

saying things I don't mean
like *I want to return* or
I cannot go on

this, I suppose, is how the heart quiets itself
by mouthing a song it does not believe.

New Year

lift the car-sharks from under their
bellies and drag them to another
sphere, crumble the husks
of every building until the debris
becomes dust, face across the black
scab that is left behind and wire-
walk into a year that is
new, that is filled with the odor of
a memory you haven't lived—
balloon both of your lungs
until they fail
until they fail

until they fail
to know
that they have
known
another
life.

Minor

so you feel small so you dangle like stray thread against the backdrop of the night the red lit night the night club light with the same pounce and tremble that made you tremble for all these years through the whiskey years and the childhood years and—now—the sober years and your hand fumbles with itself with no companion no cigarette or shot or glass just the hollow in the cusp of your hand your trembling hand and you come home in some cab some yellow cab some sitcom cab some fixture from the dreams of your youth your unsettled youth where the coming years appeared as trains thundering trains that would tremble and tilt and settle and calm the unsettled and make you feel less small.

Post Card

—there was the time that a
row of houses all agreed to
put up Christmas lights in
May. and the student body all
drank keg beer under the
bubble lights for a week. and
the copper blondes would
stroll in herds from house to
house. and the same noise
would loop every half hour.
and the end of night was only
a return to the next night.—

Post Card II

it's summer, already and
already, it's almost August.
and I wonder what Autumn
will feel like—not look or
smell or sounds like—but
what I will tell myself in the
mornings as I get on the
subway or what nightmares
will wake me from the heart
of a sleep or what little defeat
will keep me from the clasp of
my sheets, leave me in a
frantic pace between the
living room and the kitchen
and the bathroom,

half expecting some
new room that will
sit me on its cold
lap; tell me there
is more, more than
just this.

Cotton

we'll call the character Lewis

    he rummages through notebooks
    that have survived a decade in
    storage. the pages smell of moth
    balls and cardboard. there was
    an essay that he wrote in tenth
    grade about
    he desperately tries to remember
    a line that he had written about
    the green light, about how we
    all have green lights and what
    at that time was his own.

    once in a while he will look out
    into the Manhattan afternoon
    from his apartment and startle
    that this was his life. not in any
    horror or delight, just little things:
    like the color of his bedding or
    those he now called his friends. it
    felt like one day he had abruptly
    woken to all this but no one would
    confirm that it was out of place.

    what good did it do to notice how
    different years can be from each
    other. how the body of one can
    resemble so little the body it was
    torn from.

maybe that line   —the one about the green light
                  from his essay on The Great Gatsby—

was simply Lewis saying: we turn our heads backward
                                          to understand how we got
                                          here.

                                  leave a trail of cotton,
                                  shoot flares into that sky
                                  along the way.

Pact
for Hala

I want to say that I know
your story well, to tell you
that I have studied the stretch
of this calendar, carved in
pen marks and anecdotes.

I have months too. have
seen the spine of the Pacific
bellow to its severed sibling.
and what I want to say is simply
that if ever this cord is cut,
know that you will not plunge,
that our pact is no pact at all.

rather,
bring it to the Atlantic
and hear it tell you
that it is happy
to be alone.

How I Got Sober

I don't remember much of that year except that I had just gotten sober and all of Manhattan felt to me like a new world with less color and more light, and I'd spend my nights in a studio apartment in Brooklyn with all the windows closed watching sitcoms and wondering if I should catch a meeting, and when I'd finally leave the apartment it was only to get cigarettes or junk food and I never really thought I'd ever stay sober and I told that to someone at a meeting in an old church one time, before I finally stopped going to them, and he told me that the trick is to fool yourself into leaving one day and entering another and so that's what I did until one day I woke up and I'd been sober for a year, and I told myself I was done and I told myself I had done it and
I had.

Autodidact
For Layal

remember when you were thirteen
and it felt like no one could see you
so you stayed up every night of the
summer staring in front of a
computer screen thinking of how
you wanted to reinvent yourself and start
smoking and grow your hair out and
pierce your ears and laugh less and
be serious and sullen and not as silly—

     all the world is not what you thought:
     I wish you'd never learned to sulk—

     or gotten as good
     at telling yourself
     that you are
     no good

Savannah

the spite of old country
        charm   bites down in thonet rockers and curl.
        the hurling dreams of April:

like looking upward to find
        Spanish moss. tiara.

tinsel storefront.

all the grit of an intersection.

I have seen the scape of this town. the dull green canopy
        of its streets reaching out from either end
        to hold onto to one another.

        you said something about listening
        instead of performing:

        I have done both.

sugar cube. pollen. my
own skin reddened
from dry heat.

        it didn't bother me.

I walked under that pale green, looked straight up at
the Savannah sky

        told myself: you don't fool me.
           I know
           you are happy.

Babeldom

a Pashtun farmer tills the
red soil of this land. he can
hear a siren, it booms across
the colony. the workday
is complete.

the farmer joins the other
laborers, drifts into their
procession. altogether,
trample earth beneath their
feet, until a dirt storm
begins to rise

a silo behind them. he
walks with the men
back to the sleeping
camps. the cough from
his lung falls against a
shirt he binds across
his mouth.

the bed is a blanket
on a tar floor. all that
he owns fills a small
box. he rigs a pair of
pants against the wall
to use as a pillow.

this dream is a slum world
the farmer sees behind his
shut eyes. he keeps them
closed until he can see
himself digging in a field:

it is mud. it is
dirt. then—it is
stone. what he
exposes is red or blue
or a color he hasn't
yet seen. he cups
it in his palms.

the farmer cannot
decide whether
to hide this stone
in his pocket or
return it to the
soil.

in every vision
before he sleeps—the
farmer buries it back
into the ground.

wait for me,
he tells it,
I will unearth you
in my life
and not
in this dream.